My Virgo Moon

Elizabeth Stone

Presentation by *BookLeaf Publishing*

Web: www.bookleafpub.com

E-mail: info@bookleafpub.com

ISBN: 978-93-95087-64-3

First edition 2022

For Peter, Lilah, and Penny.

ACKNOWLEDGEMENT

I'd like to thank my close friends and family who have always made me feel like my words were worthy of being heard,

my cats for keeping me company in the dim hours writing by candlelight when sleep evades me,

and the world for being simultaneously so enchanting yet devastating.

The real writing comes in these moments of realization.

I thank you, reader, for feeling, at least to some degree, the same ways I do.

May we all continue seeking magic in the mundane.

Do the Days Pass by in Blues or Grays?

I feel like a puff,
a cloud in the sky;
drifting aimlessly

                                in the breeze.

Letting myself be guided by the motion
of the mind,
my soul in divine timing with the tilt

                                of the planet,

the undeviating rotation of the axis.

We are but gusts of indigo;
whispers of sapphire;
smoky cobalt;
satiny silver.

The crystalline silk of a full moon shimmers and
I'm blinded by its elegance.

To exist

                                on the same plane

as a sphere that wields such
power -
a primal magic that influences us

                    to our collective Core.

Azure floats through the atmosphere and settles
in meadows of pewter.
An ashen rain falls on lakes of slate, midnight
currents glistening.

I am one with the waves,
feeling each and every push and pull
                              of Life.

Wilted Flowers

drooping over countertops;
petals
leaving little patterns
as they drift away

                                 from stem.

I watch as another falls,
joining the other departed
petals

                amongst candle wax and twine.

I Wish it Would Snow

The sun shines too bright.

It deceives -
rays that reach out
in the guise of warmth,
until you feel ice
scraping cheeks.

                              Snow is more honest,
it says exactly what it means.

      Crystals that whisper all their secrets.

Snow and stars are within the same family,
shared wavelengths of rarity.
All sparkle
in their own unique way, nonpareil parts of a
collective.
Hearts shimmering on sleeves -
yes,

                              snow is more honest.

The Drumbeat of my Heart

coincides with the whispers of the stars in the
sky.

I used to think that rapid, anxious pace was
normal,
but I've become accustomed to this soft twinkle.

The gentle melody of
songbirds waking up,
the rhythmic nuzzling
of waves to shore.

Life is easier when one lives

slowly,
led by the circadian cycles of the
Sun and the Moon.

Indelible Words on Waning Ink

We are in the Age of Freedom,
everything is Here and Now.

I have never felt quite as in control of my life as
I do in this period of time.

My soul is ascending;
recognizing that simultaneously
Everything and Nothing matters.

An owl hoots in the night;
a champagne pop against the sky.
A reminder to be present -
you know that constellations still exist?

Life can be spellbinding;
always has been,
always will be.

A whisper in the background of my mind;
an independent bookstore,
a typewriter with the faintest amount of ink…
"This place is spellbinding, and I feel at home."
The click of keys against gnawed fingernails.

Someday maybe it will be me, behind the
independent bookstore,
the owner of the typewriter in the basement,
the one to read the offerings,
the one to replace the ink when inspiration flows
further
than technology allows.

I am an Old Soul and my Essence is exhausted.

I crave a serene existence;
let me immerse myself in books and the stories
of other characters.

Let me exist in storytelling, making the world
sound beautiful.

I Live for Floral Symbolism…

The secrets peonies keep,
the hope found in primrose.

A tulip declares its love -
hopelessly, utterly,
in the Spring,

while the hollyhocks perfume their abundance
over barren fields.

I yearn for the eternal bonds of honeysuckle,
the peace of freesia.

Protea sparks desire in my soul.

Today I Read My Tea Leaves

Dots surrounding a crescent moon,
stars speckled against dimming sky.

A sign - a gentle nudge -
to listen to dreams and intuition.

It will all pay off in the end, the dots silently
chant,
stars whirling through steam.

The moon symbolizes the most intimate part of
oneself,
the innermost feelings,
the Ethos.

My moon is in Virgo,
I know what I'm doing, she croons.
She keeps me safe and grounded,
a gut feeling like no other;

she holds my Solar Plexus in her swaying
embrace.

The Cat with the Third Eye

My Anja chakra is overactive,
my imagination in a constant state of buzzing,
a hive full of tiny ideas.

My heart counts in beats of "ohm."
My glasses fog in indigo haze.
My aura perfumes in waves of jasmine and
vetiver; I latch on to sapphires and labradorites.

My vision is blurred from years of observing,
my internal mind sees its detachment
from the external world.

I live within my fantasy, all that exists is what
my mind's eye has created.

I see a design, a fine line drawing, a cat with a
third eye.

I see myself in the ink.

Deep Sleep Haiku

Fuck, it's so early -
Why the hell am I awake?
Write this down, Mind prompts.

Betwixt Chapters

I always welcome these 5 a.m. wake-up calls,
where day is on the horizon
but the stars are still shining.

Walking the line between

                           Present and Future,
the current dusk and looming dawn; a
commentary on

                                     Time.

How seamless the change is on the surface -
the unbounded intricacies occurring

                       beyond what the eye can see.

Infinite stars for infinite outcomes, all melting
into daybreak.

The sunrise whispers secrets only the clouds can
hear.

11:11

Four repeating numbers,
numerology of the skies.

A message from the mystics,
a buzzing in the ears -
Creativity

                                                whispered

through winds of angel wings,
                1111 belongs to you.

I check the clock,
the rune chimes back at me.

I made wishes as a child,
little

                                          manifestations
                                          of magic.

Wishing words into existence,
weaving meaning from ancient wool.

Ocean eyes

                                      staring into Time,
I feel the rhythmic flutters.

"11:11, make a wish," I sill recite,
a mantra of bumblebees hovering over
wildflowers,

                    fields of marigold manifesting from

                                     mist.

Night Falls So Suddenly

The blackest of blacks blanketing the horizon;
the inky fade into credits flashing,
swirling into

                              oblivion.

There's a comfort in a sudden nightfall,
the atmosphere saying
                             "hush."

The world smells different in the dark,
olfactory glands absorbing the permeating
aromas of clean and crisp and wondrously bitter.

Snow looms somewhere on the outskirts,
anxiously awaiting its debut -
a warm light to guide in the
                             dark.

Star Charts

He has a warmness I've never felt before;
blood heating beneath the wrap of skin,
the veil of embrace.

Our signs are aligned;
double Earth, Sun and Moon,
Water Rising.

We move in ways of waves and phases, waxing
with the satellites.

The rise and fall of his chest against my
eardrum;
breathing deepened with dreams.

You Love Me

despite my chipped tooth, my overwrought
nature,
the way I live inside my head

because my hair flows like waves of seawater
and you say you adore my mind.

Dreams Have Been More Vivid

Simultaneously lucid yet real,
a dream world I know exists within my
subconscious,
yet I feel in my bones I've been there

before.

A paroxysm of sleep,
feelings that feel so real.

A house with a layout I know without knowing,
an omen
I can't seem to shake.

Time is an illusion, moments once sporadic now
all melting together.
I feel it in my dreams, know it to be true,
but the concept slips

away

during waking hours.

I wish I could hold it, to pull meaning like
puppet strings, but it always
floats back,
into the

abyss.

From a Key West Candlemaker

I have a Sylvia Plath candle,
bought at some gift shop.

Smells like "baked bread, gardenia, and old
books," it says.
I wonder, is "baked bread" a morbid joke?

I strike a match and watch it flicker in brown
glass, florals wafting through air.

The label peels at the corners,
wax spilling over.

Poetry lifts in mists and I feel it inside me -
"…sung me moon-struck, kissed me quite
insane."

I, too, am a mad girl in love.

Lyrics bloom in tulips and lovers,
living dolls of literature.
"I should have loved a thunderbird instead…"

Fire and Air, the breeze sways the flame.

I touch ink-stricken fingers to weathered pages,
I write in tiny travel journals.

100% Soy Wax.

Her words still burn on.

Gutter Cat

We found her in the gutter,
a nest made of leaves.

Calloused paws scraping against asphalt, the
weathered mews of a forty-year smoker
emerging from her raggedy little body.

She kneads at concrete,
squints at us.
The queen of the scrap metal Yard.

"Who's my little ragamuffin girl?" I trill,
"Who's my fruit bat baby?"

She slowly blinks back.

I pick ticks from her fur,
apply medication to her ears.

Her motor runs, full-volume, as she devours
food from tin cans.

Pâté in the moonlight.

Now she lives by heated blankets,

radiator days,
squeezable snack tubes.

Her adopted sister grooms her,
they play in hallway shadows.

She basks in Cincinnati sunlight
seeping through open windows,
queen of the microfiber Purple Chair.

She stretches in lazy weekend leisures, claws
piercing couch cushions.
She scratches her face on doorframes, she mews
silently as she enters rooms.

My Familiar

You growled over chicken bones,
you slept in broken dresser drawers.

You greeted with throaty chirps,
locked eyes beyond windowpanes.

You burrow under blankets, guarding over
nightfall -
clear quartz against my heart.

You gnaw on raw crystals, river rocks;
an embodiment of Dalmatian jasper,
patchwork coat against quilts.

Your Essence is a napping lioness
squinting against sunlight.
Blue calcite in the sky.

You stalk cotton balls, feathered fronds;
you pounce on catnip pouches.

You sing melodies during meal preps, full
moons -
my little kitchen witch.

Your purrs heal old wounds.

Two of Cups

I pulled the Two of Cups;
love,
friendship,
union.

A trust,
a partnership;
collaboration of
the Soul.

Respect of the other's divine, we are of equal
hearts.

Parallel lines;

                               we walk together.

Tarot of the Cat People:
"The cat's head looks over each figure."

Freya continues on her chariot, purring into
Love and War.

Three Little Musings

1. A baby pink record player, autumnal sounds scratching through Air. A mug of tea in the same shade; my periwinkle muse; Lavender Earl Grey steeping in afternoon haziness. I exist in these pastel tones; salmon cameras, rosy throw pillows. Romantic, flowery, whimsical. Soft, muted, serene. Dianthus dreamily peek up from console table vases; woolgathering within garden beds. Film develops under a blush lens.

2. Ladybugs land on Summer windowsills, they crawl over leather notebooks - they bring luck on their wings, a guest to all houseplants; they drift from the fingers of wishers. The dandelion of insects, they too wander through the winds.

3. I'm a Pothos trailing foliage, durable but dramatic. "Look at us," we say, "but leave us alone, also" - we may droop but we always bounce back. I propagate clippings; watch roots grow in clear test tubes and empty sake jars. We share a certain sense of resiliency, an understanding of how to grow with the flow. Relentless, a Pothos perseveres, vines encapsulating all surroundings, reaching toward

daylight. Variegations bursting out of macramé hangers, spilling over terracotta pots.

Am I A Recluse?

Or do I just love thinking, dreaming, being…

"In Winter in my Room"

He says I remind him of Winter.
My planets are a balance of Earth and Fire,
grounded yet pyretic.

I read wizened Dickinson poems,
I recite them into journals.
Calligraphy against acrylic paint…

frayed edges,
pressed flowers.
What would she say of my penmanship?

I'm a frosted window,
a morning breeze in November.

Moving by the moon of my September Soul.

I crave cozy chill;
the quiet after snowfall.

"A soul admitted to itself -
Finite infinity"

Hours move as minutes,
alone in my Room.

Bury me in books and buttercup blooms,
melting into Earth with
Snow.